YOUR GROWLING GUTS

and DYNAMIC digestive system

FIND OUT HOW YOUR BODY WORKS!

Paul Mason

WAYLAND

www.waylandbooks.co.uk

CONTENTS

HUMAN BODY BASICS

There are seven things you have in common with every single living creature – from plants to parrots, snakes to sea lions. All living things breathe, eat, excrete, grow, move, feel and reproduce. These are the seven 'life processes'.

Smallest parts

All living things are made of tiny building blocks called cells. All cells have the same basic parts, but the exact structure of each cell depends on the job that it does in the body. Cells are so small that they cannot be seen without a microscope.

Tissues and organs

Tissue is formed by lots of the same type of cell joining together. Types of tissue connect together to form organs. Different organs connect together in systems.

Body systems

Your body systems take care of different life processes. These include moving around, thinking, breathing and digesting food.

smooth muscle cells

Smooth muscle cells join together to form smooth muscle tissue.

Layers of smooth muscle tissues join together with other tissue types to form the stomach.

The stomach is a large organ in your digestive system. As food passes through this system, nutrients are taken out for your body to use.

YOUR GROWLING GUTS

Did you realise that you are basically hollow? There's a tube running **RIGHT THROUGH** your body! It starts in your mouth and finishes at your bottom. The tube is your digestive system. Food and drink go in one end, and something much less pleasant comes out of the other.

BRILLIANT BODY FACT

In your lifetime, your guts digest nearly 100,000 meals!

Is it really just a tube?

Not really, no. When you started life it was a tube. But as your body grew, your digestive system got more complicated. It developed muscular walls for moving food downwards. It widened in places, to form your stomach and large intestine. Little valves appeared, to stop food travelling the wrong way through the system. It also developed loops of tube that link to your circulatory system.

What is a digestive system for?

Your digestive system takes nutrients from food and passes them on to your circulatory system, for distribution to cells around the body. These nutrients are used for energy, movement, growth and repair of damaged parts. Having got as much useful material as possible from your food, your digestion also gets rid of anything that isn't needed.

STRANGE BUT TRUE!

An average person from a wealthy country eats roughly 50 tonnes of food (that's 25 adult white rhinos!) during their lifetime. They also drink about 50,000 litres of fluid.

How does it work?

The first stage is for food to be broken into smaller pieces, which move more easily through the system. (If you've ever swallowed a too-big mouthful, you'll know why this is a good idea.) This process is called mechanical digestion.

At the same time as your food is broken into smaller pieces, chemical digestion starts. Chemicals called enzymes speed up the breakdown of food into smaller and smaller parts. Finally, the nutrients from food are small enough to pass into the blood.

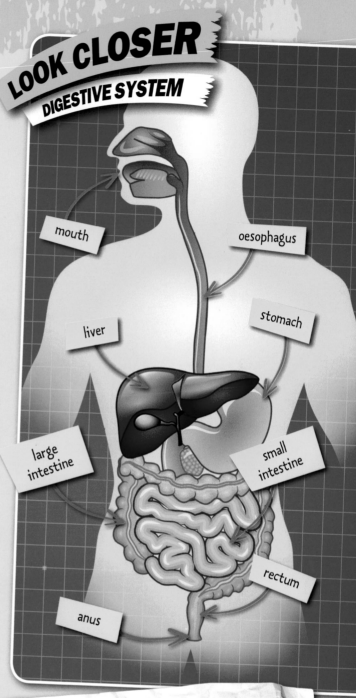

mouth

oesophagus

liver

stomach

large intestine

small intestine

rectum

anus

Digestion begins in your mouth, when you chew food.

DID YOU KNOW?

Thin people don't have smaller stomachs.

There is no relation between how thin you are and the size of your stomach. Everyone's stomach is around the size of a fist and stretches depending on what is put into it.

See for yourself

How much can a stomach hold?

Find a 2-litre bottle. This holds the same volume as a completely full adult stomach. Now put 5 tablespoons of water into the bottle. This is about 75ml - which is the average volume of a completely empty stomach.

It's a big difference!

THE MIRACULOUS MOUTH

Your mouth is the arrivals hall for your digestive system. Mind you, the guests don't get a very friendly welcome. They're smashed up by your teeth and swirled around in saliva, before being swallowed down a dark hole. It's a good job they are only bits of food!

Rough guide to the mouth

You may not think much about your mouth – but there's actually a lot going on inside it. A thin bony plate called the hard palate separates the mouth from the nasal passages. The soft palate is flexible and is important for swallowing and breathing. Lips are important for all kinds of things, including speech, allowing food into your mouth, and keeping it there while you're chewing.

LOOK CLOSER
MOUTH PARTS

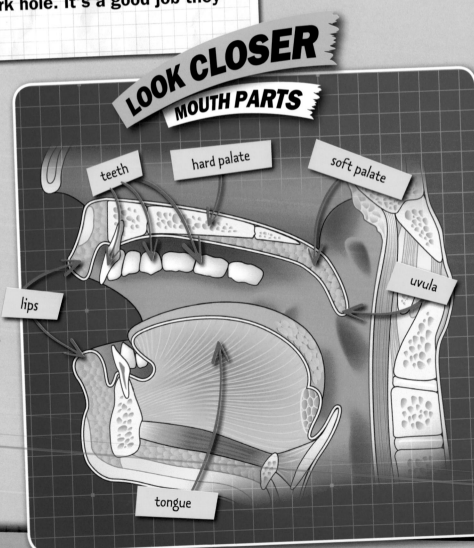

teeth

hard palate

soft palate

lips

uvula

tongue

A close-up of the surface of the tongue.

The tongue

The tongue is an organ made mainly of muscle. Along with the cheeks and lips, it is used to control food while chewing and keeps food in place so that it can be ground up by the teeth. The tongue is coated with a mucous membrane (a layer of slimy material), which helps stop microbes entering the body.

The mouth and taste

Scientists say there are four basic tastes: sweet, salty, sour and bitter. Your tongue is covered with nerve endings called taste buds. Together, the taste buds send a message to your brain about what you are eating. They also sense the temperature of food and its texture.

Hotel bacteria

An ordinary mouth contains well over FIVE HUNDRED different types of bacteria. In total, there can easily be more bacteria in someone's mouth than there are people on Earth (which is 7 billion and rising). Some bacteria are harmful; others are helpful.

The average mouth also contains over 70 types of fungus, and a few viruses and parasites. Yeuw.

Just a few of the billions of bacteria on someone's tongue.

No one is really sure what it's for, but touching the uvula makes you gag. It may also be important in speech and the swallowing process.

STRANGE BUT TRUE!

Scientists once thought that the ability to roll your tongue into a tube shape was inherited from your parents. This may not be 100% true. In one study, half of a group of children could tongue-roll at 6 or 7. By the time they were 12, three-quarters could do it. They had <u>learned</u> to tongue roll!

See for yourself

As well as being used when eating, your tongue is crucial for speech. Moving it about in your mouth makes it possible to form words. Testing this is simple. Just try speaking normally, but with your tongue deliberately kept pressed against the bottom of your mouth, against your lower teeth.

TIME TO CHEW

Teeth start the process of breaking food down by mashing it up as you chew. Teeth are also important for speaking – try talking without your tongue touching your teeth and you'll see!

molars

canines

premolars

incisors

How many teeth do you have?

In total, most people have 52 teeth in their lifetime. Not all at once, though! There wouldn't be room in your mouth.

Stage 1 Young children have 20 teeth by the time they are about three years old. These are called baby teeth, or primary teeth.

Stage 2 New teeth, growing behind, start pushing the baby teeth out when you are about six years old. By about 12 years old, most children have 28 new teeth.

Stage 3 In their 20s, most people get four more teeth, called wisdom teeth. So adults with all their teeth have 32 in total.

Are all teeth the same?

No – and each type of tooth in your mouth has a specific job to do. At the front of your mouth you have incisors and canines. These are used for biting into things, from apples to burgers. The incisors slice into food, while canines grip and tear. Further back in your mouth are premolars and molars, which are used for chewing. This breaks your food down into pieces small enough to be swallowed.

STRANGE BUT TRUE!

No two people have exactly the same teeth. The marks left behind when you bite something are as unique as fingerprints. Some criminals have even been identified from their bite marks!

LOOK CLOSER
A TOOTH

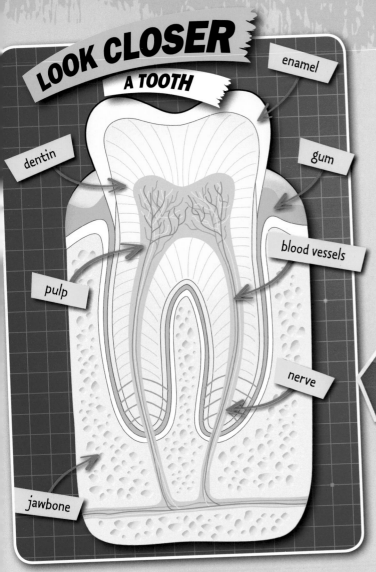

enamel

dentin

gum

blood vessels

pulp

nerve

jawbone

DID YOU KNOW?

Your mouth waters for a reason.

Saliva does an important job in digestion. It mixes with food in your mouth, helping to break it down. It also acts as a lubricant, helping the food to slide down your throat when you swallow.

Saliva also washes the chemicals in food into your taste buds. Without saliva, you wouldn't be able to taste what you are eating.

DON'T TRY THIS AT HOME!

In the past, people with toothache often visited a barber to have the painful tooth removed (there were no trained dentists back then).

One way to remove a tooth was with a 'tooth key'. The 'key' end was placed over the tooth, the 'handle' was turned, and with luck, the tooth popped out. If you were unlucky, the tooth shattered and the pieces had to be plucked individually from your bleeding jaw.

What are teeth made of?

Teeth are not hard all the way through. Under the hard outer crust that you see when someone smiles, there are several more layers. Enamel – on the outside – is the hardest tissue in the body. A softer layer called dentin sits under the enamel and is the second line of protection if the enamel cracks. The hard outer layers protect the pulp – this is full of nerve endings and blood vessels and is VERY painful if touched!

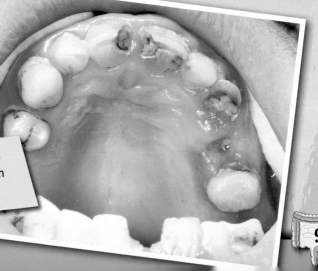

The bacteria that cause tooth decay like this double in number every 4–5 hours. How often do you think you need to clean your teeth?

JOURNEY DOWN THE OESOPHAGUS

The oesophagus is sometimes called the 'food pipe'. It is a muscular tube that passes food from your mouth to your stomach. The oesophagus works a bit like a boa constrictor swallowing its prey!

The art of swallowing

Once your teeth, tongue and saliva have got your food to just the right consistency, it forms into a little ball, or bolus. You don't have to think about this, it just happens.

The bolus gets pushed to the back of your mouth and is swallowed down the oesophagus. The oesophagus's muscular walls expand ahead of the bolus and contract behind it, forcing food down. This muscle action is called peristalsis. Food always moves in just one direction – which makes it possible to drink a glass of water while standing on your head.

LOOK CLOSER
PERISTALSIS

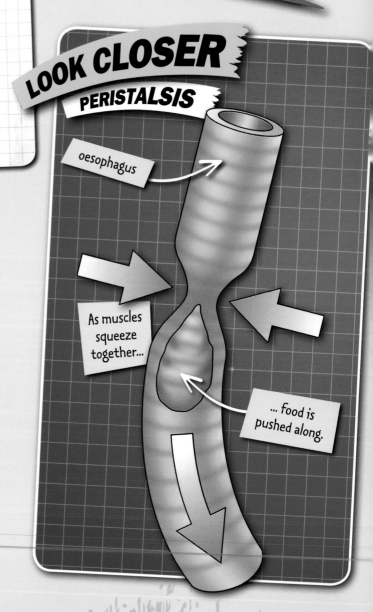

oesophagus

As muscles squeeze together...

... food is pushed along.

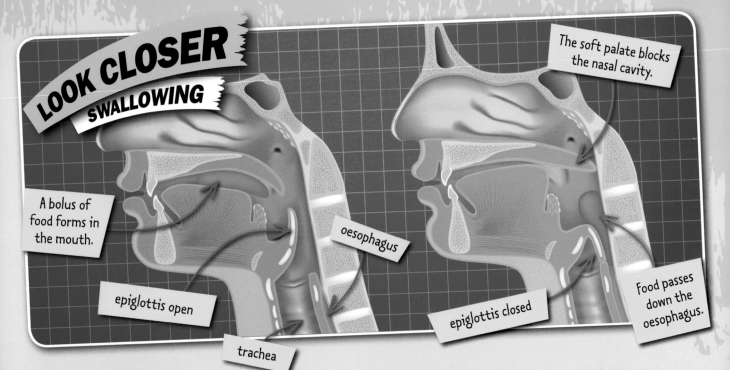

A bolus of food forms in the mouth.

oesophagus

epiglottis open

trachea

The soft palate blocks the nasal cavity.

epiglottis closed

Food passes down the oesophagus.

The epiglottis

The oesophagus shares your mouth's rear exit with another tube, called the trachea or windpipe, which leads down to your lungs. When you swallow, a flap called the epiglottis covers the trachea's opening. This stops food entering your trachea and blocking it, or even getting into your lungs.

Usually the epiglottis does its job perfectly – but food can sometimes get trapped in someone's windpipe. This blocks the airway and stops air getting to their lungs. If the food is stuck for more than a few seconds, the person could suffocate.

DO TRY THIS AT HOME –

but only in an emergency!

If someone gets something stuck in their windpipe, the blockage needs to be dislodged as quickly as possible. Call loudly for help from an adult.

If the person is over the age of one, get him or her to lean forward onto your hand. Use your other hand to strike them on the back, between the shoulder blades, using the heel of your hand. Do this up to five times – it may dislodge the blockage.

STRANGE BUT TRUE!

'Oesophogastroscopy' is a big word for having a look at the inside of the oesophagus and stomach. The first oesophogastroscopy was almost certainly performed in 1868, when an inquisitive German doctor named Adolf Kussmaul examined a professional sword swallower.

THE BODY'S FOOD MIXER

Once it has been swallowed, food is squeezed all the way down the oesophagus and into the stomach. This is like a stretchy bag of muscle. Here, mechanical digestion AND chemical digestion happen.

The food churner

Your stomach works like a cement mixer for your digestive system. Well, a food mixer, at least. It takes delivery of lightly chewed boluses of food from your mouth. Then the muscles that make up the stomach start contracting and relaxing, churning up the food.

This contracting and expanding to churn up food is normally just a background noise. Once in a while, though, it becomes a bit too loud for polite company! The rumbling is especially loud when you're hungry, and the churning noise echoes around inside your empty stomach.

LOOK CLOSER
STOMACH

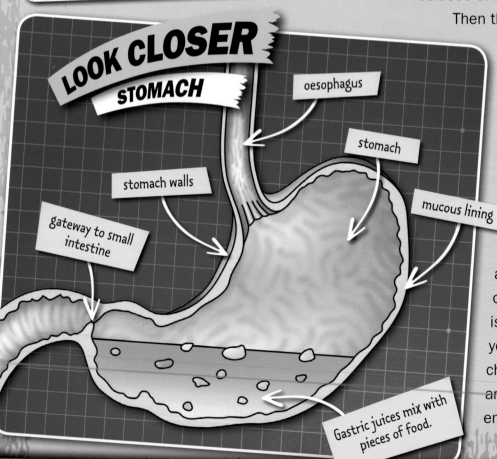

oesophagus

stomach

stomach walls

mucous lining

gateway to small intestine

Gastric juices mix with pieces of food.

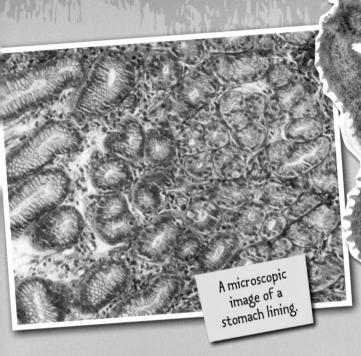

A microscopic image of a stomach lining.

Both chemical and mechanical digestion happen in other parts of the digestive system — so humans can actually survive without a stomach! But some animals don't have one in the first place. In the seahorse and platypus, for example, swallowed food passes straight into the intestines.

Acid attack! (on your food)

At the same time as it is churning food, your stomach releases acid, which helps enzymes break down the chewed-and-churned food still further. The acid is basically the same as hydrochloric acid that's used to strip rust and paint off metal. It can eat through skin, bone, and just about anything else you might swallow.

All that stomach acid helps to defend your body against some harmful bacteria, which get destroyed. But the stomach also has to defend ITSELF against the acid. It does this by producing a thick mucus lining. When the acid eats the lining away, the stomach just produces more. In the end, your stomach gets a new lining every two weeks or so.

DON'T TRY THIS AT HOME!

In 1822, a Canadian fur trapper called Alexis St Martin was accidentally shot in the side. The wound healed, but left a hole that went through to his stomach. St Martin's doctor, William Beaumont, spotted that this was a great opportunity to study digestion. He spent the next few months dangling bits of food into the patient's stomach on a bit of string, to see what happened to it.

St Martin died in 1880, at the age of 86 — still with a hole his side.

DID YOU KNOW?

If you stop eating, your stomach doesn't shrink.

Your stomach does shrink down when not in use, but as soon as some food arrives to be processed, it expands again.

THE (LONG) SMALL INTESTINE

When food leaves your stomach, it enters the small intestine. It might be CALLED the small intestine – but an adult's is about 6m long. That's over halfway up to the highest diving board in the Olympics!

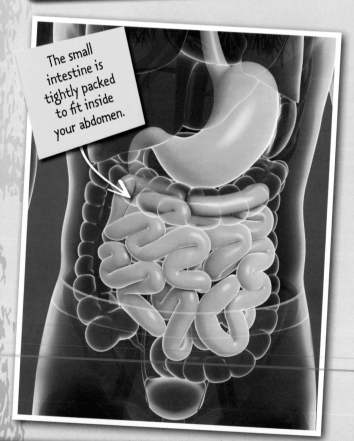

The small intestine is tightly packed to fit inside your abdomen.

Why does the small intestine need to be so big?

The small intestine is big because this is where the most important part of digestion happens. Here, your body removes about 90% of the nutrients from food. The nutrients are transferred to your blood, ready for delivery to cells around the body. To achieve this, the intestine has three separate areas:

The first part is the duodenum. This connects to the stomach. Here, chemicals containing enzymes mix with the food, breaking it down into small pieces.

The jejunum is the middle part of the small intestine, which continues the breakdown of food into its individual nutrients.

The ilium is the last part and connects to the large intestine. It is very similar to the jejunum, and is where the final nutrients are absorbed into the blood.

How do nutrients get into the blood?

The small intestine is lined with tiny structures called villi, which stick out into the tube of the intestine. Most villi are roughly 1mm long, and have even smaller microvilli sticking out from them. Inside the villi are blood vessels.

In the duodenum and jejunum, the villi are leaf-shaped. They help to release chemicals containing enzymes that break food into its individual nutrients. In the ilium, the villi are finger-like to increase surface area. Here the individual nutrients are absorbed through the walls of the villi into the blood.

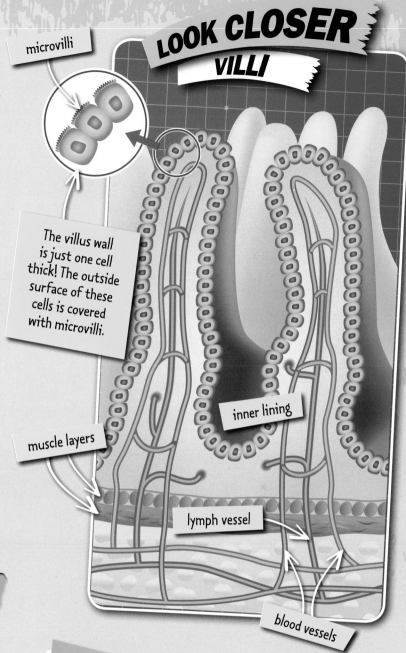

microvilli

The villus wall is just one cell thick! The outside surface of these cells is covered with microvilli.

muscle layers

inner lining

lymph vessel

blood vessels

A magnified section of the small intestine shows the inner lining.

STRANGE BUT TRUE!

The small intestine may be 6m long, but it is very thin at just 2.5cm in diameter. If it were completely smooth inside, the small intestine's surface area would be about the same as the seat of a chair. The inside of an adult's small intestine has at least the same surface area as your living room!

YOUR LOVELY LIVER

Your small intestine does not do its digestive work alone. A whole team of other organs helps the intestine to work (though these organs are usually counted as separate from the digestive system).

The liver and gallbladder

When blood leaves your small intestine, it contains nutrients. The blood travels straight to the liver. The liver is a bit like a food warehouse, where nutrients are released from the blood and processed. It filters out harmful substances, stores energy, and distributes nutrients to cells around the body.

Your liver also produces chemicals that are used in digestion. One of these is bile, which your duodenum needs in order to break down fat. The bile is stored in your gallbladder ready to be released when needed.

LOOK CLOSER
DIGESTIVE ORGANS

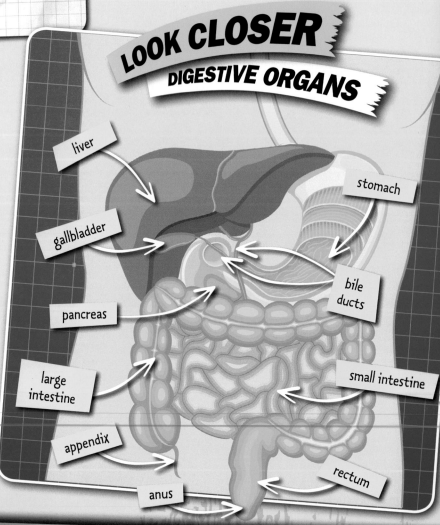

liver

stomach

gallbladder

bile ducts

pancreas

large intestine

small intestine

appendix

rectum

anus

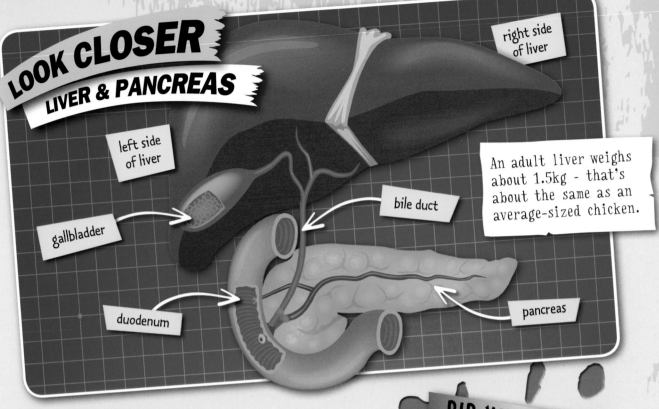

right side of liver

left side of liver

gallbladder

bile duct

An adult liver weighs about 1.5kg - that's about the same as an average-sized chicken.

duodenum

pancreas

The pancreas

The pancreas's big job is to release chemicals called enzymes into the duodenum. When food arrives in your duodenum, it has been smashed up in the mouth and churned around in the stomach. But (as anyone who has ever vomited will know) food in your stomach is not 100% liquid. So the enzymes break the food down even more so that nutrients can be absorbed into the blood.

Re-growing a liver

Your liver has an amazing ability – it can grow back. This means that part of a person's liver can be donated to someone else. A section is removed and transplanted into another person. The donor's liver just grows to almost the same size as before.

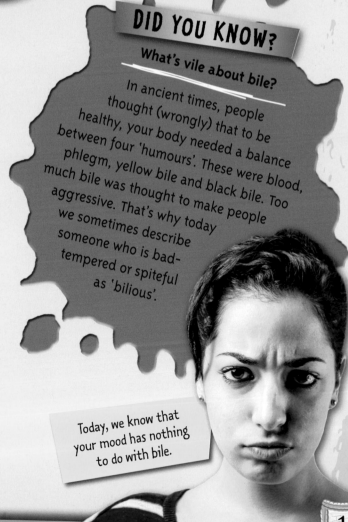

DID YOU KNOW?

What's vile about bile?

In ancient times, people thought (wrongly) that to be healthy, your body needed a balance between four 'humours'. These were blood, phlegm, yellow bile and black bile. Too much bile was thought to make people aggressive. That's why today we sometimes describe someone who is bad-tempered or spiteful as 'bilious'.

Today, we know that your mood has nothing to do with bile.

THE LARGE INTESTINE

Remember how the small intestine was about 6m long? How big do you think the **LARGE** intestine is? Well, it's actually only about a quarter as long, at 1.5m. It can stretch much wider than the small intestine, though, which is how it gets its name.

From liquid to solid

When food leaves the small intestine, it no longer looks anything like food. It is a kind of sloppy liquid. The liquid goes through a valve of muscle that closes tightly behind it. There is no going back now – the valve will not allow it. The liquid has entered the large intestine, where water and the last few nutrients will be removed.

As food passes down the large intestine, the body absorbs its liquid. The food sludge gradually becomes thicker and more solid. Eventually it solidifies into

LOOK CLOSER
LARGE INTESTINE

The main part of the large intestine is sometimes called the colon.

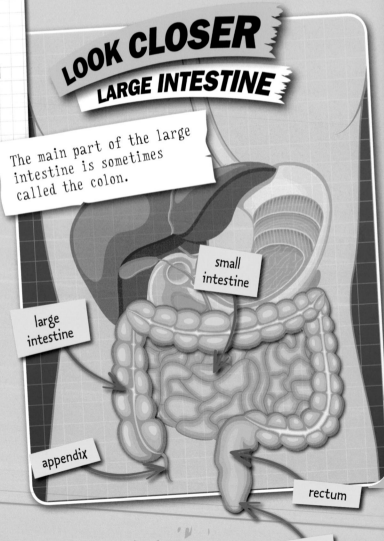

small intestine

large intestine

appendix

rectum

anus

Today, it is possible to have an intestinal transplant if you have a problem with part of your intestine. French doctor, Alexis Carrel, carried out the first trials of these transplants using dogs. He used sewing techniques he had learned from a tailor!

DID YOU KNOW?

Meat DOESN'T get stored in your large intestine.

There is an urban myth that goes something like: 'By the time they're 40, most Americans have 2kg of undigested red meat in their large intestine.' In fact, food has already been 90% digested by the time it reaches the large intestine. The rest of the nutrients it contains are removed within hours – whether you are American or not.

stools. This isn't the kind of stool you want to sit on, though – it's another word for faeces, or poo. The stools pass into the rectum and finally, pass out of your anus when you go to the toilet.

Microscopic helpers

Living inside your intestines is a crowd of microscopic helpers, called bacteria. In your large intestine, one of the jobs of these microscopic helpers is to break down any undigested food. They also attack any harmful bacteria that have managed to get this far, and even help train your body to fight off disease. The only bad thing about them is that they do produce gas – find out more on the next page...

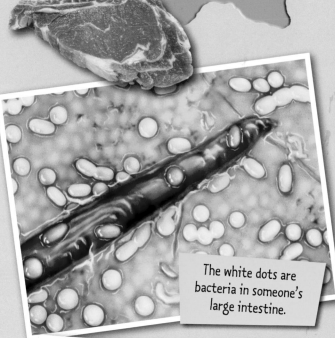

The white dots are bacteria in someone's large intestine.

STRANGE BUT TRUE!

Right at the start of your large intestine is a little side-passage called the appendix. Doctors do not really know what it is for. One theory is that when humans used to eat tree bark and grass, they digested it in the appendix.

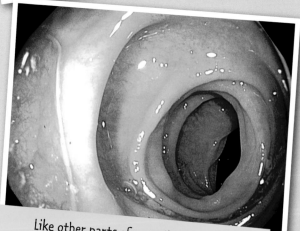

Like other parts of your digestive system, the large intestine is lined with muscles that contract to move food through.

DIGESTIVE WIND

There are over 700 different kinds of bacteria in your large intestine. In total, your guts contain roughly 100 trillion (100,000,000,000,000) microscopic bacteria. That's more or less TEN TIMES the number of cells that make up your whole body!

Bacterial jobs

Each type of bacteria has a job, and many produce things your body needs. The most important are useful vitamins. Bacteria also break down fibre – hard-to-digest plant matter. While doing their work, the bacteria make by-products that the body needs to get rid of.

Intestinal gas

One of the bacteria's by-products is gas. Inside your body, this gas is called intestinal gas. It mixes with other gases that have been swallowed into your digestive system. To avoid blowing up like a balloon, your body needs to get rid of this gas. In fact, on average people need to get rid of about half a litre of gas every day.

As it leaves your body, the gas changes its name to 'wind' (or flatulence). Wind is usually about 58% nitrogen, 21% hydrogen, 9% carbon dioxide, 7% methane and 4% oxygen. The remaining 1% contains sulphur – which is usually what makes it smell.

Tiny, gas-producing bacteria are hard at work in a large intestine.

STRANGE BUT TRUE!

In France, a performer called Le Pétomane was popular before the First World War. Le Pétomane is French for 'The Fartomaniac'. His act involved playing instruments, blowing out candles, and even blasting out songs – using wind from his bottom.

Breaking wind

Many people claim never to break wind, but they do, to release the gas that builds up in their intestines. Most of the time the gas passes out in small quantities and doesn't smell – so you don't notice. When it does smell, or there is more of it, it is probably to do with what you have eaten.

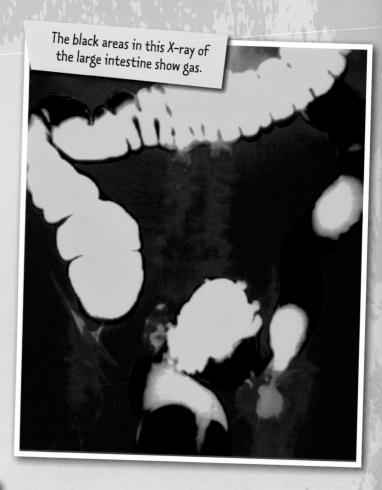
The black areas in this X-ray of the large intestine show gas.

Whatever they tell you – EVERYONE breaks wind.

See for yourself

NOTE: Do NOT do this experiment if you are likely to be in a confined space with other people.*

*Handy hint: Your wind can be smelt 10-15 seconds after release. Plenty of time to move away, or claim that the dog did it.

The food you eat affects the smell of your wind. Food containing sulphur will make it smell worse, because of the gas produced by sulphur-seeking bacteria. These foods include beans, onions, cabbage, cheese and egg. Try some, and assess the results.

DON'T TRY THIS AT HOME!

An Ancient Roman emperor named Claudius (10BCE–54CE) passed a law saying that breaking wind was allowed at banquets. Claudius thought holding it in was bad for you. (Even today, doctors don't agree on whether he was correct or not.)

More recently, in 2011 Malawi's Minister of Justice suggested that breaking wind in public should be made illegal. People found the idea so laughable he had to withdraw it.

DIGESTIVE WASTE:
STOOLS

Your body is brilliant at getting the maximum possible nutrition from your food. By the time it reaches the end of the long intestine, all that's left are things your body does not need. This has formed into solid lumps called stools – which lots of people call poo.

How fast is your digestion?

The answer is different from person to person. It depends on the kind of food you eat. People whose food contains a lot of fibre are usually quicker. If your food is short on fibre, it takes longer to pass through. On average, food takes twice as long to be processed in wealthy countries, where people eat less fibre.

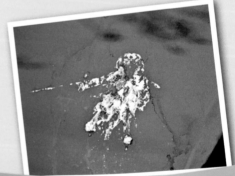

DID YOU KNOW?

In Ancient Rome, not everyone had their own toilet.

Many people used public ones. These were very sociable - there were no barriers, so you could sit and chat to your neighbour!

STRANGE BUT TRUE!

Bird poo is partly white because birds can't urinate. Instead, their bodies mix poo (the black bit) and wee-sludge (the white bit) together.

Questions answered

People often have lots of questions about poo, but are embarrassed about asking them. So here are some answers!

How often should you go? There is no correct answer to this question, because everyone is different. However, as long as you normally go between three times a day and four times a week, you are in the normal range.

What makes stools smell? The blame lies with the same bacteria that make your wind smell. As they break down food, the bacteria produce by-products, some of which stay in your stools.

Why are stools brown? Stools get their colour from the red pigment in red blood cells called bilirubin. When red blood cells die, a lot of the pigment they contained ends up in your intestines – and then in your stools.

What your stools say about you

You can learn quite a lot from your stools. The shape, size and colour all give clues about your diet and digestion. In fact, there is even an international chart to help analyse stools, called the Bristol Stool Chart. Numbers 3 and 4 are the healthiest!

DON'T TRY THIS AT HOME!

Constipation is the name for when you need to let out some stools, but can't. It can be painful and upsetting, but today it is easily cured with drugs or other treatments. Things were not always that way — crazy constipation cures from the past included:

* squirting a quarter litre of yoghurt up someone's bottom

* swallowing mercury (a liquid that is actually poisonous)

* squirting water, perfume and herbs up someone's bottom (King Louis XIV of France apparently had this done four times a day!).

BRISTOL STOOL CHART

TYPE 1		Separate hard lumps, like nuts (hard to pass)
TYPE 2		Sausage-shaped but lumpy
TYPE 3		Like a sausage but with cracks on its surface
TYPE 4		Like a sausage or snake, smooth and soft
TYPE 5		Soft blobs with clear-cut edges (passed easily)
TYPE 6		Fluffy pieces with ragged edges, a mushy stool
TYPE 7		Watery, no solid pieces – entirely liquid

PROCESSING LIQUIDS

To stay alive, you need to drink fluid as well as eating food. In fact, although most food's main component is water, some would claim drinking is more important than eating. You can stay alive for weeks without food – but only a few days without fluid.

Fluid's jobs in your body

The water your body gets from drinking and processing food is important. Water makes up the biggest part of your blood, helps your joints to move, and is essential for keeping your brain working properly. Your body also uses water to flush away waste products.

The kidneys and bladder

Waste products are cleaned out of your blood by your kidneys. You have two kidneys. They combine the waste with water, making urine. The urine passes down two tubes called ureters to your bladder. When empty, an adult's bladder is about the size of a pear. As it fills with urine, it expands. A full bladder can be the size of a small melon!

When your body senses that your bladder is full, your brain gets a message saying it's time to go to the toilet. When you get there, muscles in your bladder relax, two valves open, and the urine flows out.

LOOK CLOSER
KIDNEYS

Your kidneys make urine, which is then stored in your bladder.

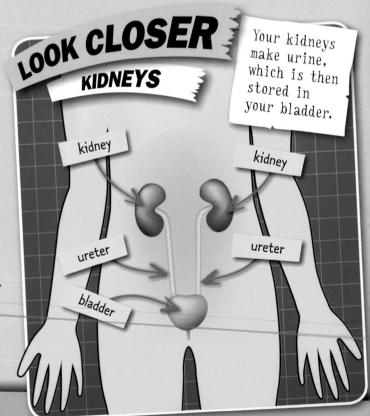

kidney

kidney

ureter

ureter

bladder

24

What your urine says about you

It used to be common for doctors to sniff, or even SIP, a patient's urine as a way of discovering what was wrong with them. So, what can your urine reveal about you?

① Colour

Normally, urine should be a pale yellow colour. If it gets darker, this shows that it contains more waste products and less water. So darker-yellow urine probably means you are not drinking enough.

② Smell

Urine does not normally smell strongly. If your urine smells sweet, or like bleach, it may be a sign that you should visit the doctor. (If you have been eating asparagus, though, wait a day: it makes most people's urine smell strange.)

Urine can be used to test for health problems.

DON'T TRY THIS AT HOME!

In Ancient Rome, people rubbed wee into their teeth to make them whiter. Wee contains a chemical called ammonia, which DOES bleach the colour out of things — so this treatment should actually work! Today, though, there are much less unpleasant ways to get whiter teeth.

STRANGE BUT TRUE!

Some foods can affect the colour of some people's urine — but this isn't true for everyone. Some people might experience the following:

* reddish urine from eating loads of beetroot
* dark brown, or even black urine from eating fava beans or rhubarb
* pink urine from eating blackberries.

beetroot

rhubarb

blackberries

VOMIT AND
OTHER PROBLEMS

Sometimes, your digestive system has a problem and wants to get rid of its contents fast. When this happens, there are only two possible escape routes: at the top of your digestive system, or the bottom.

The norovirus – also called the 'vomiting bug'!

Vomiting

If your body detects something in your food that's bad for you, you may have to vomit. People also vomit for other reasons, including eating too much, feeling very scared, motion sickness, and illness caused by harmful microbes such as viruses or bacteria. Whatever the cause, you don't usually have much choice over when you vomit. When you vomit, an emergency message from your brain tells the muscles in your digestive system to go into reverse. Instead of pushing food down, they force it rapidly up to your mouth – and out.

YOU CAN'T TRY THIS AT HOME!

In 1968, Neil Armstrong and Buzz Aldrin became the first humans ever to set foot on the Moon. Like typical tourists they left a few things behind when they went home, including footprints that are still there today and a US flag on a pole. They also left behind a bag of vomit, caused by space sickness.

Diarrhoea

If something upsets your large intestine, it too gets rid of its contents – often very quickly. This terrible urge to sit down on a toilet and go is called diarrhoea.

LOOK CLOSER
VOMITING

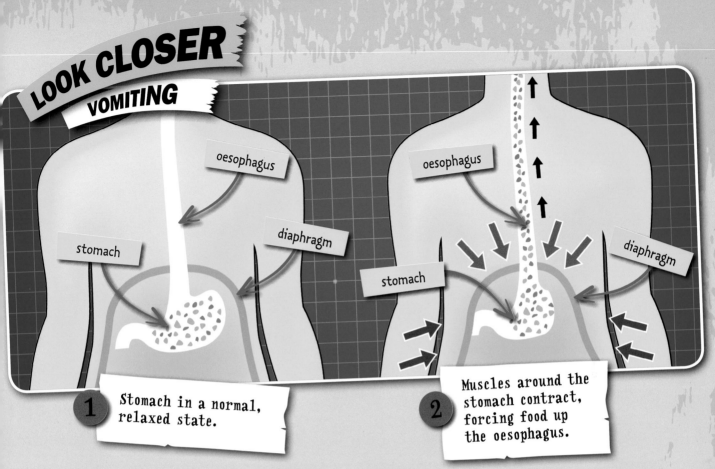

1 Stomach in a normal, relaxed state.

oesophagus

stomach

diaphragm

2 Muscles around the stomach contract, forcing food up the oesophagus.

oesophagus

stomach

diaphragm

A virus is usually responsible, but diarrhoea also happens if food contains poisonous bacteria. Your body senses the problem and acts quickly to get rid of it.

When you have diarrhoea, your body speeds up the process of getting rid of your stools. To do this, it increases peristalsis in the large intestine. The water that would usually be absorbed here is hurried on, making your stools watery and soft. Then the muscles of your large intestine contract to force the stools out.

DID YOU KNOW?
Ancient Rome and the vomitorium.

Ancient Romans are said to have had 'vomitoriums'. These are said to have been rooms where people at a feast could go to vomit up what they'd eaten and drunk. Then the vomiters could go back and carry on with the party.

The 'vomitorium' DID exist — but it was actually a kind of large passageway in a theatre or amphitheatre, which allowed lots of people to arrive or leave quickly.

STRANGE BUT TRUE!

Sperm whale vomit and stools sometimes contain a valuable substance called ambergris, which was once used in making perfumes.

Only about 1% of sperm whales produce ambergris, and very little of what is released is ever found. It's not surprising that perfume makers have now found alternative materials!

MAINTENANCE
AND SERVICING

People eat all sorts of different foods. Strange snacks from around the world include fried spiders (Cambodia), lime-and-garlic grasshopper (Mexico), and even rotted shark (Iceland). Our amazing digestive systems cope with them all!

small enough to swallow. Unfortunately, your mouth is full of bacteria, which eat the little bits of food that get left behind. As they do this, the bacteria release plaque on to your teeth. Unless it is regularly brushed off, the plaque eats away at the teeth and eventually destroys them.

Digestive troubles

Even though your digestion can cope with spicy spiders or fried grasshopper, it is not indestructible. If you eat the wrong foods or are unwell, your digestion can stop working properly. The most common problems are pain in your abdomen, constipation and diarrhoea. So, what are the best ways to keep everything digesting properly?

 ## See for yourself

Before you brush your teeth in the morning, scrape them with your nail. Have a look at the white stuff that has been scraped off: that's tooth-attacking plaque. Imagine how much would build up if you didn't brush your teeth for 24 hours.

Brush your teeth

Your teeth are the first stage of your digestion. You need them to smash your food into pieces

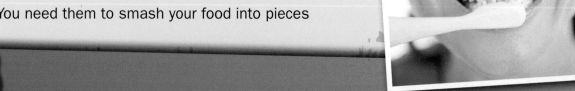

A BALANCED DIET

Plenty of fruit and vegetables: these contain vitamins and minerals, which are vital for health, and also provide fibre.

Plenty of foods such as bread, rice, potatoes and pasta: these provide carbohydrates (which your body uses for energy) and nutrients.

Some milk and dairy foods such as cheese or yoghurt: these provide protein, which your body uses for growth and repair work, and calcium to keep your bones and teeth strong.

Some meat, fish, eggs and beans, which contain protein, vitamins and minerals.

Only a little (if any) cake, sweets and fizzy drink.

Eat a healthy diet

This is important for two reasons. Firstly, a healthy diet will help keep your digestion working properly. Secondly, a healthy diet contains all the nutrients you need for your body to grow and work properly.

Drink, drink, drink

Water is important in the digestive system. Most people need to drink at least a litre of fluid every day to keep theirs working properly. Exactly how much you need to drink depends on how big you are and what you eat. This is because you also get fluid from your food. Water and milk are the healthiest drinks.

DID YOU KNOW?

Fruit juice and brushing teeth don't mix.

You should avoid drinking fruit juice if you are about to brush your teeth. The citric acid in fruit juice weakens your teeth's protective coating for about half an hour. If you brush your teeth in that time, you will be brushing away the teeth's protection!

GUTSOME WORDS!

abdomen the part of the body containing your digestive organs, basically from the bottom of your ribs to your hips

absorb to soak up or take in, like a sponge soaking up water

bacteria tiny living organisms made up of a single cell. Bacteria in your body do lots of useful jobs, particularly in digesting food, but some types of bacteria can also cause illness.

blood vessel a tube that carries blood around the body, for example to and from the heart or other organs

bolus a ball of chewed food and saliva that is swallowed when you eat

by-product something that is produced as a side-effect, for example, when you boil water, you also get steam

carbohydrates types of sugars that the body uses for energy, they are contained in some foods

cell the smallest building-block that a living organism can be made of, usually only visible under a powerful microscope

circulatory system the system that moves blood around the body, made up of blood vessels and organs such as the heart

enzymes the chemicals that make a process inside your body happen, or happen more quickly. In your digestive system, enzymes are important for breaking food down so that your body can use it.

fibre a type of food that is able to survive attack by human digestive enzymes, which means it does not break down inside your body

lubricant usually a liquid or semi-liquid that makes it easier for one object to slide past another

microbe a microorganism that exists as just one cell, and can only be seen with a microscope

mineral a non-living natural substance, for example iron. Your body needs certain minerals to stay healthy.

motion sickness the feeling that you are about to be sick, or actually being sick, as a result of travelling

mucus a protective coating and lubricant produced in various parts of your body

nutrient a substance in food that is used by the body to keep working and for growth and repair

peristalsis the squeezing movement made by muscles to move food through parts of the digestive system, such as the oesophagus and the small intestine

pigment a type of natural colouring found in animal or plant tissue

urban myth a story that is told as though it is true, even though it seems unlikely (and is not true)

virus a tiny living organism that lives inside the cells of other organisms, and can cause diseases

vitamin a particular kind of nutrient, needed in very small amounts for your body to work properly and grow

DIGEST THIS INFORMATION

Are you hungry for extra information about your digestive system? Here are some good places to find out more:

BOOKS TO READ

Infographic Top Ten: *Record-Breaking Humans,* Jon Richards and Ed Simkins, Wayland 2014

How to Build a Human Body, Tom Jackson, Scholastic 2013

Mind Webs: *Human Body,* Anna Claybourne, Wayland 2014

Truth or Busted: *The Fact or Fiction Behind Human Bodies,* Paul Mason, Wayland 2014

WEBSITES

http://kidshealth.org/kid/htbw/digestive_system.html

This website is a really good place to find out all sorts of information about the human body. It has an excellent section on the digestive system.

http://www.childrensuniversity.manchester.ac.uk/interactives/science/bodyandmedicine/digestivesystem/

The Children's University of Manchester, UK, has all sorts of information for kids, presented in the form of labelled illustrations. It includes this section on the digestive system.

PLACES TO VISIT

In London, the **Science Museum** has regular exhibitions and displays explaining how the body works. The museum is at:

Exhibition Road
South Kensington
London SW7 2DD

The Science Museum also has a good website:

www.sciencemuseum.org.uk/whoami/findoutmore

The **Natural History Museum** has an amazing 'Human Biology Gallery' where you can find out all about your amazing insides and how they keep the body working. The museum is at:

The Natural History Museum
Cromwell Road
London SW7 5BD

The museum also has a good website:

http://www.nhm.ac.uk/visit-us/galleries/blue-zone/human-biology/

INDEX

WAYLAND

First published in Great Britain in 2015 by Wayland
Copyright © Wayland, 2015
All rights reserved.

Dewey Number: 612.7-dc23
ISBN: 978 0 7502 9243 6
Library ebook ISBN: 978 0 7502 9244 3

10 9 8 7 6 5 4 3 2 1

Editor: Annabel Stones
Designer: Rocket Design (East Anglia) Ltd
Consultant: John Clancy, Former Senior Lecturer in Applied Human Physiology
Proofreader: Susie Brooks

Wayland
An imprint of
Hachette Children's Group
Part of Hodder & Stoughton
Carmelite House
50 Victoria Embankment
London EC4Y 0DZ

An Hachette UK Company
www.hachette.co.uk

www.hachettechildrens.co.uk

Printed in China

Artwork: Ian Thompson: p10, p12; Ian Thompson/Stefan Chabluk p8 tr; Stefan Chabluk: p6, p9 tl, p15 tr, p23 br, p24, p27 t.

Picture credits: Getty Images: p22 bl LTL / Contributor; iStockphoto: p5cl , p7 bl, p13 cr; Science Photo Library: p3 ct, p13 tl CNRI, p19 cr BO VEISLAND, MI&I, p19 br GASTROLAB, p20 bl CNRI, p21 tr LUNAGRAFIX, p26 ANIMATE4. COM; Shutterstock: p3 t, p3 cb, p3 b, p4, p5 r, p5 br, p7 t, p7 cr, p7 br, p8 bc, p9 br, p11 t, p11 bl, p11 br, p13 tr, p14, p15 bl, p16, p17 t, p17 br, p18, p19 tr, p21 cl, p21 bl, p21 cr, p22 br, p25 tr, p25 bl, p25 bc, p25 br, p27 br, p28 cl, p28 br, p29 all; Wellcome Library, London CC Wikimedia Commons: p9 cr. Graphic elements from Shutterstock.

YOUR BRILLIANT BODY

Marvel at the wonders of the human body with this fact-packed series.

978 0 7502 9388 4

978 0 7502 9246 7

978 0 7502 9240 5

978 0 7502 9237 5

978 0 7502 9249 8

978 0 7502 9243 6

Find out more about the human body with other Wayland titles:

978 0 7502 7868 3

978 0 7502 8158 4

978 0 7502 8241 3

978 0 7502 8280 2

SAINT BENEDICT CATHOLIC
VOLUNTARY ACADEMY
DUFFIELD ROAD
DERBY
DE22 1JD